THE
WORK
REDESIGN
TEAM
HANDBOOK

A Step-by-Step Guide to Creating Self-Directed Teams

Darcy Hitchcock

QUALITY RESOURCES®
A Division of The Kraus Organization Limited
One Water Street, White Plains, New York 10601

AQP **Association for Quality and Participation**
801-B West 8th Street, Cincinnati, Ohio 45203

Copyright © 1994 Axis Performance Advisors, Inc.

Printed in the United States of America

98 97 96 95 94   10 9 8 7 6 5 4 3 2 1

Quality Resources
A Division of The Kraus Organization Limited
One Water Street
White Plains, New York 10601
914-761-9600
800-247-8519

The paper used in this publication meets the minimum requirements of American National Standard for Information Sciences—Permanence of Paper for Printed Library Materials, ANSI Z39.48-1984.

ISBN 0-527-76243-1

Library of Congress Cataloging-in-Publication Data

Hitchcock, Darcy E.
   The work redesign team handbook / Hitchcock.
      p. cm.
   Includes index.
   ISBN 0-527-76243-1 (alk. paper)
   1. Self-directed work groups--Handbooks, manuals,etc. I.Title
HD66.H58 1994
 658.4'02--dc20   94-8914
                                                      CIP

Contents

Introduction vii

1 Get Ready 1

2 Conduct Technical Analysis..................................... 11

3 Conduct Social Analysis 23

4 Combine Ideas 39

5 Formalize Recommendations 47

6 Formalize Related Changes 57

7 Troubleshoot the Plan 63

8 Develop a Detailed Implementation Plan 67

Appendix... 73

    Recommended Reading 73

    Blank Worksheets... 77

Index.. 102

Introduction

"Organizations are perfectly designed to get the results they get."

—Arthur Jones

Welcome to the *Work Redesign Team Handbook*. A work redesign team (commonly referred to as a design team) is a temporary task force of employees who have been assembled to analyze the workplace and recommend changes that are necessary to achieve self-direction. These design teams often struggle, confused about what to do and how to do it. This handbook is intended to help design teams make decisions concerning the implementation of self-direction. It presents an eight-step process and explains how to use a number of analytical tools within each of these steps.

WHERE DESIGN TEAMS FIT IN

When organizations implement self-directed teams, they usually go through three phases:

1. Establishing a plan.
2. Getting teams up and running.
3. Aligning systems and linking to others.

In the first phase, a steering committee is usually formed to manage the entire process. They establish the plan, make decisions that will affect the entire organization, and procure the resources to carry out the implementation. The steering committee usually includes high-level managers who can ensure that adequate commitment and support is available. Some steering committees represent a diagonal slice through the organization because they include members from all areas and levels of the organization. If your organization does not have a steering committee, you may want to assemble one. Otherwise, assume that the management team to which you report is operating as your steering committee.

As part of the second phase, the steering committee usually appoints design teams—temporary task forces of front-line employees—to make decisions for their specific work group. These design teams identify opportunities to improve their own performance and employee satisfaction and make recommendations to the steering committee. This handbook provides direction for these design teams.

The design team may recommend changes to organizational systems such as compensation or information systems. These recommendations are generally acted on in the third phase.

WHO SHOULD USE THIS HANDBOOK

Ideally, each member of the design team should have a copy of this handbook. This ensures that everyone has access to the information and knows what to expect from the meetings. This also enables team members to share the responsibility of facilitating the design team meetings.

Although this handbook is targeted at design team members, steering committee members may find it helpful in understanding what to expect from the design teams.

Managers and human resource professionals who are beginning to explore self-directed teams have also found the handbook useful because it identifies issues and tasks they will encounter if they decide that self-direction is appropriate for their organization.

HOW TO USE THIS HANDBOOK

This handbook should be used by the design team members to plan and conduct their meetings. Design teams should use this handbook as a flexible guide, adapting the tools and steps to their individual needs.

Before convening, the design team should scan the handbook to get an overview of the process. Then, before each meeting, the persons responsible for running the meeting should review the relevant content in the handbook and plan how to facilitate the meeting. The blank worksheets provided at the back of the handbook can be used to prepare visual aids such as overheads or flip charts for use during the meeting. Those responsible for facilitating the meetings should also assemble any additional materials such as flip chart markers, masking tape, and the like.

Each activity can be conducted at varying levels of detail. The design team will need to use its own judgment concerning how much analysis will be fruitful. Try to invest your time wisely, going into the most detail where the team feels the analysis will yield the biggest payback. If the team gets bogged down, ask yourselves if you have gone past the point of diminishing returns and consider redirecting the process. Be aware, however, that moderate amounts of impatience and frustration are normal.

This handbook is intended as a resource and should not be expected to replace effective consulting or support. Ideally, design teams should have access to people who understand organizational development and socio-technical systems design. This is especially important for so-called ''greenfield'' sites (new sites that are being designed from the ground up as opposed to ''brownfield'' sites where an existing workplace is redesigned). Typically, greenfield sites will probably need to conduct a more thorough analysis using more rigorous socio-technical systems design methods and will certainly want to get additional assistance beyond the scope of what this handbook can provide.

Design team members are encouraged to read reference material on the theory and practices of organizational design. The team might want to assign reading material to individuals on the team and have them report on what they have learned. (See the Recommended Reading in the Appendix of this handbook.)

HANDBOOK ORGANIZATION

The *Work Redesign Team Handbook* is divided into the eight steps you should complete:

1. Get Ready.
2. Conduct Technical Analysis.
3. Conduct Social Analysis.
4. Combine Ideas.
5. Formalize Recommendations.
6. Formalize Related Changes.

7. Troubleshoot the Plan.

8. Develop a Detailed Implementation Plan.

Each chapter or step contains these sections:

- *Overview* of the step.
- *Decision Checklist* to help you select the most helpful tools and analyses.
- *Team-Building Activity* to kick off each meeting and unite the team.
- *Tools and Processes*, which explains how to use each tool.
- *Output*, which describes how you should summarize the results of the step.
- *Follow-Up* actions you should take.
- *Preparation for Next Steps*, which describes what you should do to get ready for the next step.

BEFORE YOU BEGIN

Before you begin meeting, you should familiarize yourself with this handbook and make sure you have all the necessary information for Step 1, Get Ready. In particular, be sure you have answers to these questions from your steering committee:

- Who should be on the design team? The design team should be composed of respected members of the affected work groups, representing all positions or functions. They should be selected on the basis of their technical knowledge and experience, communications skills, leadership ability, and interest in making teams work.

   We recommend the steering committee get guidance from their human resources department or corporate attorney concerning the composition and charter of the design team. At the time of this writing, it is unclear what impact the recent National Labor Relations Board rulings will have on the selection and use of design teams.

- What is the charter of the design team, its purpose, constraints, boundaries, expectations, deadlines, and resources? What can the team make actual decisions—versus only recommendations—about? What will be done with the recommendations, and what criteria will be used to evaluate options?

- What education should the design team members receive on self-direction before the first meeting, and how will they get that training?

- Has a hand-off list (describing the responsibilities the teams can assume) been completed, and what are the hand-offs?

- Are there certain leadership roles all teams should have?

- How is the design team expected to communicate with the steering committee?

- How will the design team find time to meet? How often will they meet? Is overtime approved?

- Who will facilitate the design team meetings? Options include using an outside facilitator (such as an internal consultant), the leader of the work group, or all design team members.

- Why is the organization implementing teams? How do teams help the organization address its strategic needs? What is the relative priority of the reasons?

- What subject matter experts should be involved in the design team process?

- Who on the steering committee will kick off the first design team meeting?

PURPOSE, TOOLS, AND OUTCOMES

The following chart summarizes the purpose, tools, and outcomes of the eight steps of the design team process.

Step	*Purpose*	*Tools*	*Outcomes*
1. Get Ready	Establish expectations	Design team charter Meeting ground rules	Design team plan
2. Conduct Technical Analysis	Find opportunities to improve how work is done	Process diagram Work flow diagram Deliberations analysis Variance matrix	Cost/benefit analysis

(continued)

Step	*Purpose*	*Tools*	*Outcomes*
3. Conduct Social Analysis	Identify opportunities to leverage human potential	Network diagram Responsibility chart Leadership roles diagram Team assessment	PMI (Pluses, Minuses, Interesting) chart and organizational options Inconsistent practices
4. Combine Ideas	Find the best combination of ideas from steps 2 and 3	Weighted criteria chart Interrelationship worksheet	Associated changes
5. Formalize Recommendations	Add detail to the approved ideas that relate to team membership and roles	Sign-up sheets Responsibility matrix Leadership roles worksheet Training plan	Implementation timetable
6. Formalize Related Changes	Add detail to the remainder of the approved ideas	Weighted criteria chart PMI chart Cost/benefit analysis	Proposal worksheet Action plan
7. Troubleshoot the Plan	Find the bugs	Dry run simulation	Solutions to identified problems added to plan
8. Develop a Detailed Implementation Plan	Make sure you have thought of everything	Implementation checklist Communication plan	Completed implementation plan

1

Get Ready

"Would you tell me please, which way I ought to go from here?" "That depends on where you want to get to," said the Cat.

—Alice's Adventures in Wonderland

The first meeting of a design team should be kicked off by a member of the steering committee. This session should introduce all members to their purpose and to the eight steps. If a steering committee member is not able to conduct this session, the design team leader should get the information needed to handle step 1.

OVERVIEW

A steering committee member should begin the meeting by explaining the charter of the design team and reviewing the reasons for implementing self-directed teams. The eight steps should be reviewed, and meeting roles should be established. Depending on individual needs, it may be helpful to conduct a team-building exercise and establish ground rules. By the end of this step, the design team should have finalized a charter and formalized a plan for completing the eight steps.

DECISION CHECKLIST

Using the decision checklist shown in Figure 1.1, identify the most important tools and processes for your design team to perform during this step.

1

FIGURE 1.1 *Decision Checklist for Step 1*

✔ = This analysis would be useful
✕ = This analysis may NOT be useful; use another tool

If you have:	Design Team Charter	Meeting Ground Rules
• No document that describes the design team's purpose, mission, expectations, constraints	✔	
• Design team members who are not used to working together		✔
• Had trouble working together in the past		✔
• No established meeting ground rules		✔
• Been given a completed charter from the steering committee	✕	

TEAM-BUILDING ACTIVITY— STANDARDS OF EXCELLENCE

This is the first of a recurring team-building activity. These activities are intended to help unite your team while addressing issues related to your redesign effort. In each of the eight steps, we will provide you with a question to pose to the design team members. Write this question on a flip chart and ask each person to jot down his or her answer. Allow one or two minutes for contemplation. Then ask each person to share his or her answer. After all have shared their answers, summarize the common themes or comments under the question on the flip chart.

When you pose the questions, don't worry if you do not generate content that can be used in that specific step. The main purpose of these activities is to encourage understanding, trust, and openness among the team members. Use them as a 10-minute ice breaker at the beginning of each meeting.

Figure 1.2 provides the questions for each step. There is a question for each of the eight characteristics of effective teams. Feel free to change the questions or replace this suggested team-building activity with another.

FIGURE 1.2 *Team-Building Activity Questions*

Step	Category	Question	Purpose
1	Standards of excellence	If you could pick one person who embodies the values you want this organization to embrace, who would that be and why?	To identify shared hopes and values
2	Shared goals	What are the three things your external customers most want, and how does your work group contribute to those key quality characteristics?	To focus the team on customer needs
3	Supportive systems	Think of an organizational system (e.g., business planning, purchasing, or compensation) that does not support quality and teamwork. How could you see that system being changed?	To provide input for the inconsistent practices chart
4	Competent members	What is a skill that you have only used away from work that could be an asset in our new organization?	To reveal the untapped talents of employees
5	Collaborative climate	Think of an interaction that actually occurred in this team or organization that you think should be handled differently in the future. How did the interaction violate the values you identified in step 1, and how should similar situations be handled in the future?	To reveal additional training or support needed to implement a team-based culture
6	Results oriented structure	If you could spend a week working with someone, following him or her around, who would that be and why?	To reveal needs for information channels, learning, opportunities, changes to structure

(continued)

FIGURE 1.2   (continued) *Team-Building Activity Questions*

Step	Category	Question	Purpose
7	Committed staff	In your new team organization, if you were able to hire the next executive, what characteristics would you look for in the applicants?	To glimpse the far-reaching effects of this organizational change
8	Effective leadership	If you could ask one person in the organization to do one thing to demonstrate commitment to this change, who would you ask and what would you ask him/her to do?	To generate ideas for a communication plan

TOOLS AND PROCESSES

Setting the Stage

The meeting should be kicked off by a member of the steering committee. This should be conducted as a two-way exchange of information to negotiate roles and boundaries. The content should include:

- Why the organization is implementing self-directed teams.
- How the design team members were selected and why.
- What the design team's purpose, expectations, and constraints are.
- Who will facilitate the design team meetings.
- How the steering committee sees themselves supporting the design team's efforts.

Design Team Charter

A charter puts in writing the purpose of the team. It helps clarify the mission and expectations. There are many ways of formatting a charter. The example we provide in Figure 1.3 can serve as a guide if your organization does not have a standard format for such documents. A charter should include:

- A mission statement that clearly states the reason the team has been formed.

- Indicators of success that identify for all stakeholders what success would look like when the mission is accomplished.

- Key result areas the team should focus on to achieve success.

FIGURE 1.3 *Sample Design Team Charter*

MISSION:

Making us partners in the business

Following the eight-step design team process, the manufacturing design team will recommend the best combination of technical and social changes for the Widget Plant to maximize work performance and employee satisfaction.

INDICATORS OF SUCCESS:
- Our owners will receive a return on the investment of at least 50% on self-directed work teams within two years.
- All employees feel challenged and satisfied from their work.
- We will have no EPA incidents.

KEY RESULT AREAS:

Research and Development:
- We must be open to creative uses of new methods and technologies, even from other industries.
- We must involve subject-matter experts within our own organization.

Sales and Marketing:
- We must be sensitive to the impact our recommendations may have on other groups, especially our customers.
- We must regularly communicate with and involve our work groups and the steering committee.

Production or Core Work:
- We must complete all tasks thoroughly, honestly, and openly to get the most accurate information from our team members.
- We must strive to go beyond our individual interests and be willing to change. We must eliminate unnecessary steps in our process and demeaning or bad jobs.

Administration:
- We must establish effective methods to keep track of and communicate our analyses, options and decisions.

To complete a design team charter, follow these steps:

1. Gather information for the mission statement. Each member of the team should complete these sentences and jot their ideas on a piece of paper.

    *   We exist to (achieve what result) . . .
    *   For (what work groups) . . .
    *   By using (what techniques or steps) . . .
    *   Within (what boundaries or constraints).

2. Write their ideas on a flip chart. Then refine the ideas, eliminating unnecessary words and maintaining the most important concepts. Write the final mission statement. You may want to include an inspiring motto or phrase that encapsulates your hopes for this effort.

3. Identify all your stakeholders. Stakeholders are people or groups that have a vested interest in what you are doing. These may include the owners, management, employees, customers, other work groups, regulators, and others.

4. For every stakeholder group, write at least one success indicator, a condition that will indicate you have met their needs. For instance, a success indicator for employees might be that ''The knowledge, expertise, and interests of all employees are leveraged'' or ''All employees find satisfaction in their work.''

5. Now identify key result areas. Key result areas are functions that are critical to your success. Teams usually have key result areas in four areas; you should adapt these to your needs:

    *   Research and Development—Learning about new technologies, methods, or tools.
    *   Sales and Marketing—Learning about your stakeholders' and customers' needs, expectations, desires, and complaints.
    *   Production/Core Work—How you go about completing design team work.
    *   Administration—How you will manage your work and keep track of the information you generate.

    List key result areas under each of these four categories. For instance, you may list under Production that ''Our team meetings must be managed so that all design team members feel free to speak openly about their concerns, ideas, and needs.'' Under Research and Development, you may determine that ''We should identify the best emerging technologies to give us a leg-up on our competitors.''

Meeting Ground Rules

Ground rules are agreements teams make about how they will conduct themselves. They may include procedural elements (e.g., start on time and rotate role of time keeper) as well as interpersonal (e.g., there are no dumb ideas and speak up if you disagree).

To create ground rules for your design team, follow these steps:

1. Hand out packs of 3″ × 3″ adhesive-backed notes. Have all team members complete these sentences, writing only one idea per page:

   - As a member of this design team, I am worried/concerned that . . .

   - It irritates me in meetings when . . .

   - I might stop coming to design meetings if . . .

2. Post flip charts with these three headings: procedural issues, interpersonal issues, other. Ask participants to post their comments on the appropriate chart.

3. Break the design team into three groups and assign each group a flip chart. Each group should analyze and cluster the comments into categories. Then each group should write a ground rule that might alleviate the problems raised by the comments.

4. Have each group report on their results.

5. Consider each suggested ground rule separately. Ask if everyone would be able to agree to it. Ground rules that everyone can accept should be posted on a separate flip chart entitled Meeting Ground Rules.

6. Explain that everyone is now responsible for making the design team follow these rules. The ground rules should be a ''living'' document—that is, the design team can add to or delete from the list later as needed.

7. If not already covered in the ground rules, make sure you have addressed these issues:

   - How often will the design team meet and how long will the meetings last? Where will the meetings be held and how much of an interval between meetings is appropriate?

- What meeting roles will be assigned? Who will facilitate, take minutes, record ideas on a flip chart, keep track of time, and monitor group process? After the meetings, who is responsible for communicating with work groups and with the steering committee?

OUTPUT

By the end of this step, all design team members should understand what they are to accomplish, should be willing to work together, and should have agreed to ground rules for the meetings. These are usually encapsulated in a design team charter and meeting ground rules document.

Design Team Plan

You should also formalize a design team plan that lays out your expectations for what you will complete in each meeting and when you expect to complete each of the eight steps. Figure 1.4 shows a sample design team plan.

Follow these steps to complete a design team plan:

1. List all the tasks you plan to complete under each of the eight steps along the left side of the plan. Cross out any tasks or tools which are unnecessary. A listing of all the tools and outputs is in the Introduction.

2. Decide how many meetings each task may take.

3. Write appropriate time references along the top of the chart (e.g., weeks, months).

4. Identify the tentative meeting dates by drawing a line next to the step under the appropriate time reference.

5. Analyze your plan. Have you forgotten anything? Are the time frames reasonable? Track your progress on the plan and adjust it as necessary.

FOLLOW-UP

Share your charter and design team plan with your work groups and the steering committee. Explain how you want them to participate in this design process and what support you may need from them.

FIGURE 1.4 *Sample Design Team Plan*

Step	Tasks	July Week 1	Week 2	Week 3	Week 4	August Week 1	Week 2	Week 3	Week 4
1. Get Ready	Design team charter	|							
	Team building activity	|							
	Ground rules		|						
	Design team plan		|	|					
2. Technical Analysis	Process diagram				|				
	~~Work flow diagram~~								
	~~Deliberations analysis~~								
	Variance matrix					|			
	Cost/benefit analysis					|			
3. Social Analysis	Network diagram					|			
	Responsibility chart						|		
	Leadership roles diagram						|		
	Team assessment							|	
	PMI charts							|	
	Inconsistent practices								|

PREPARATION FOR NEXT STEPS

Review Step 2, Conduct Technical Analysis, and decide which tools you will use. Gather any existing documents that might help you complete step 2 (e.g., blue-prints or process diagrams).

Identify and invite any subject-matter experts who might be helpful in your technical analysis. They may include engineers, systems analysts, researchers, or retired workers.

2

Conduct Technical Analysis

"A fool . . . is a man who never tried an experiment in his life."

—Erasmus Darwin

You should begin the redesign process by examining the technical aspects of your work, identifying opportunities to improve the process and methods before examining the social aspects of work. In this way, you avoid redesigning around an inefficient process. For example, Mazda reengineered their accounts payable system so that many steps in the process were eliminated. Instead of invoices and purchase orders passing in the mail, Mazda automated the process. Now, when an order is received at the dock, the computer matches the request with the delivery and automatically cuts a check. Vendors have been asked not to produce invoices. Mazda employees probably would not have come up with this creative solution without first analyzing their technical system in detail.[1]

OVERVIEW

In this step, you should look for opportunities to improve the quality and efficiency of your work. This may include streamlining the process and changing technology as Mazda did, or it may involve changing the methods you use or the physical layout of your space.

On the basis of your needs, you may perform one or more of these analyses:

- Process diagram—Maps all the steps in your work process.

- Work flow diagram—Reveals problems in physical layout.

---

[1]Hammer, Michael (July/Aug, 1990). "Reengineering Work: Don't Automate, Obliterate." *Harvard Business Review*, pp. 104–112.

- Deliberations analysis—Helps identify improvements to nonrepetitive, non-routine processes such as scientific research and counseling.
- Variance matrix—Lets you identify the key variables in a process that affect quality.

The final product of these analyses should be a list of possible improvements and their associated costs and benefits.

DECISION CHECKLIST

Using the decision checklist shown in Figure 2.1, identify the most important tools and processes for your design team to perform during this step.

TEAM-BUILDING ACTIVITY—SHARED GOALS

Conduct the next team-building activity. Write the question (see Figure 2.2) on a flip chart and ask each person to jot down their answer. Allow one or two minutes for contemplation. Then ask each person to share their answer. After all have shared their answers, summarize the common themes or comments under the question on the flip chart.

TOOLS AND PROCESSES

Process Diagram

The approach you take to diagramming your process depends on the nature of your work. For instance, if you are in manufacturing, you may already have schematics for your manufacturing process. (If you do, check them for accuracy.) However, in many cases, you must diagram the process yourself. The diagram usually includes the following information:

- What is being done.
- Who is doing it.
- How long it takes to perform the step.
- How long before the next step is initiated (elapsed time or down time).

FIGURE 2.1 *Decision Checklist for Step 2*

✔ = This analysis would be useful
✗ = This analysis may NOT be useful; use another tool

If you have:	Process Diagram	Work Flow Diagram	Deliberations Analysis	Variance Matrix
• Rework or redundant steps	✔	✔		
• Not recently diagrammed your process	✔			
• A need to speed up processes or reduce bottlenecks	✔	✔		
• Much time spent going from one area to another		✔		
• Regularly spent time going back and forth		✔		
• A nonrepetitive process; every time is different	✗		✔	✔
• Trouble controlling the quality of the work or identifying root causes	✔			✔
• Professionals (e.g., engineers) who have spent significant effort analyzing or improving your processes, the results of which match your understanding	✗			
• A large investment in capital expenditures (i.e., equipment or offices) that would be prohibitively expensive to change or move		✗		

FIGURE 2.2   *Team-Building Activity for Step 2*

Step	*Category*	*Question*	*Purpose*
2	Shared goals	What are the three things your external customers most want and how does your work group contribute to those key quality characteristics?	To focus the team on customer needs

You can map the process against those who perform the steps, or against time, or both. Or you can flow chart all the steps and decisions in the process. You will need to use your judgment to determine which approach would be best for you given the nature and complexity of the process.

Figure 2.3 maps the process of writing a letter using both time and performers. The myth is that the manager dictates the letter, the secretary types it, the manager signs it, and the secretary sends it out. However, when you diagram the real process, it usually looks more like this:

FIGURE 2.3   *Sample Process Diagram*

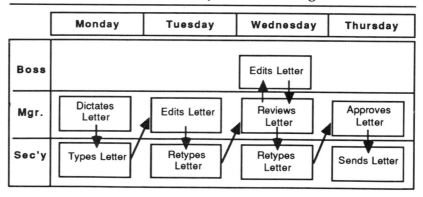

Notice how long it takes with the three *R*s: rework, revision, reviews. Usually, once a process is mapped, everyone laughs at the lunacy and then redesigns the process to be more streamlined. Figure 2.4 shows how to redesign the letter-writing process.

FIGURE 2.4 *Redesigned Process Diagram*

	Monday	Tuesday	Wednesday	Thursday
Boss	Sets Critical Expectations			
Mgr.	Types/Edits Letter			
Sec'y	Proofs/Sends Letter			

Any process really has three views:

- What you think it is.
- What it really is.
- What it should be.

When you map out a process, you must diagram what is really happening, not what the procedures manual says. Only then will you identify how to improve the process.

To complete a process diagram, follow these steps:

1. List the main steps in the process down the right side of the diagram.

2. Make a time line of appropriate duration along the top of the diagram.

3. Using action verbs, describe the sequence of key tasks for each step in the process. Using a bold line, indicate how long the task takes. Use a thin line to show elapsed time before the next step is initiated. You may need to estimate these times. Be sure to diagram how the process is actually done. Figure 2.5 shows a sample process diagram for washing clothes.

4. Analyze the diagram and identify waste in the process. This may include the three *R*s: rework, revision, reviews. You may also find long elapsed times between steps that might be shortened or eliminated.

   In the washing example shown in Figure 2.5, sorting clothes happens repeatedly. This could be resolved with separate hampers for darks and lights early in the process and for members of the family hampers at the end of the process (new methods). Because this is a batch process (i.e., you want a full load) there is a long elapsed time before beginning laundry—which is fine

FIGURE 2.5 *Sample Process Diagram for Washing Clothes*

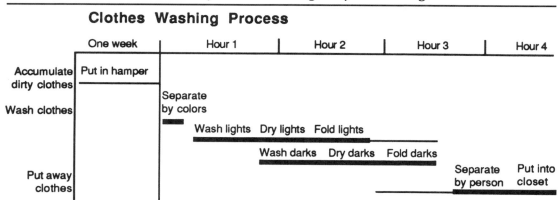

unless you run out of socks or need to get full use out of the equipment to make it pay for itself. You could change the process and wash clothes twice a week or change methods and wash your socks by hand. Another long elapsed time occurs because we own only one washer—while the lights are being washed, the darks cannot be started. If we were paying someone to do our laundry, we might be able to justify getting another washer. Come to think of it, why doesn't someone invent a washer with two compartments so you could do lights and darks at the same time (i.e., a new technology)?

You need to use judgment to determine how much detail is necessary to show on the diagram. If we had added more detail to the clothes-washing process diagram, showing additional steps such as carrying clothes up and down the stairs, we might have discovered problems with physical layout. For example, why, when most of the laundry comes from the bedroom, do we put the laundry room next to the kitchen?

5. Draw a revised process diagram to show how you think the process could be improved.

Work Flow Diagram

A work flow diagram helps identify inefficiencies in your physical layout. You might be surprised to learn how often you retrace your steps. Take a drawing of your office or site and draw lines to indicate where a person must go to complete a task or process. See Figure 2.6 for a sample diagram. Follow these steps to complete a work flow diagram.

1. Get or create a drawing of your work area.

2. For each person or position, draw lines to indicate where that person must go to complete his or her tasks. You may want to use different colored pens

FIGURE 2.6 *Sample Work Flow Diagram*

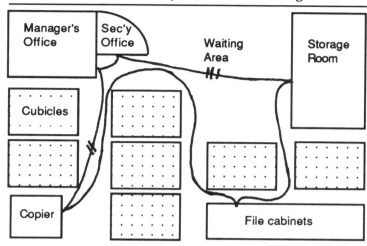

for each person. To reduce clutter, you can use hash marks to indicate multiple trips along the same path.

3. Analyze the diagram for inefficiencies. Are people going back and forth to get materials? Are people bumping into each other's areas? Does the diagram look like a plate of spaghetti?

4. Redraw an improved layout that corrects most or all of the problems you identified. You might want to lay out options on graph paper using cut-outs of furniture and equipment. Remember that teams may use space differently than traditional work groups. For instance, they need space to meet and post team data. Consider your team's special needs as you change the layout. Layout solutions include placing positions in a linear order (so that team members do not have to back-track) and putting frequently used stations (e.g., the manager's office or the copy machine) in a central location.

Deliberations Analysis

The work that some people perform is so specialized that it is impossible to identify the process to any level of detail. This is more likely to be the case with knowledge workers, such as researchers and investment counselors. In these situations, it is often more productive to examine the types of interactions or deliberations that take place and clarify the needs of all parties.

Consider an investment counselor. The counselor may follow a basic process: investigating your needs, recommending investments, and managing your portfolio. However, so many variables can affect what the counselor does that mapping the process in detail—every possible combination of variables—

would be overwhelming. Instead, it might be more fruitful to look at the types of interactions or deliberations the investment counselor has and discover what could be done to improve those deliberations.

For an investment counselor, deliberations might include a preliminary meeting with a client, a follow-up meeting with the client, ongoing communication with the client, informational meetings with investment researchers, and staff meetings. The people involved, the purpose of the meetings, and the requirements vary widely.

Figure 2.7 shows a sample deliberations analysis. To complete a deliberations analysis, follow these steps:

1. Identify all the types of deliberations that occur. These may include formal meetings as well as impromptu exchanges around the coffee pot. A deliberation is defined as ''discussions that must take place on the road to a solution, invention, discovery, decision, or plan.''[2]

2. For each deliberation, list who is usually involved and what their needs are for the deliberation. Also identify what they bring to the deliberation.

3. Identify any factors or obstacles that get in the way of effective, open communication. These may include lack of trust, insufficient information, noisy environment, and not enough time.

4. Analyze your data. Look for needs that go unmet because no one brings appropriate information to the deliberation. Discuss who should be responsible for bringing this information and add this information in a new color to your deliberations analysis. Watch for the wrong people participating in the deliberation. Also consider the obstacles to effective communication and recommend ways to overcome them.

Variance Matrix

Discovering the root cause of quality problems can often be a challenge. There may be so many steps in the process or so many variables that affect one another that it can be hard to distinguish causes from effects. One technique that helps you get a handle on this is to develop a variance matrix that shows the relationship between variables. A sample matrix for baking bread is shown in Figure 2.8.

---

[2]See reference to Cal Pava's work in Weisbord, Marvin (1987). *Productive Workplaces: Organizing and Managing for Dignity, Meaning and Community.* San Francisco, CA: Jossey Bass.

FIGURE 2.7 *Sample Deliberations Analysis*

Deliberation	Players: Needs and Brings	Obstacles	Recommendations
Initial client meeting	Client: Needs to like and trust counselor; needs to gain confidence in firm; needs to become aware of services	Client often nervous about sharing personal information	Use private office; explain confidentiality agreement. Share personal information about counselor
	Client: Brings biases, last account statement, priorities Should also bring copy of will, listing of all accounts and balances, life insurance policy, pension, spouse (if applicable)	Client often does not bring all appropriate documents	Send checklist before meeting
	Counselor: Needs to learn client's total current financial status, tolerance of risk, goals, constraints, and biases	Counselor is often in too much of a hurry to gather information, which puts off client	Spend time building trust. Ask permission to begin interviewing questions. Plan one-and-a-half hour meetings instead of just one hour. Focus on understanding their needs and situation

FIGURE 2.8 *Sample Variance Matrix*

Baking Bread

Mix Ingredients						1. Amounts of ingredients (wrong proportions)
						2. Water temperature (too hot/cold)
	2					3. Viability of yeast (too old, killed)
Knead Dough						4. Time kneading
						5. Air temperature
	1	2	3	4	5	6. Amount dough rises
Bake Bread						7. Temperature of oven
					7	8. Baking time

To complete a variance matrix, follow these steps:

1. List the major steps in the process down the left side of the matrix.

2. For each step in the process, list the key variances—that is, those items that can affect the quality of the product or service.

3. For each variance, note which other variances it can affect. Put the number of the variance in the box across from the affected variances.

4. Analyze your matrix. Numbers in a row show which other upstream variables might affect that variance. Numbers in columns indicate how the variance affects downstream operations. Look for the significant few—those rows or columns with many numbers. Notice in the example above that many upstream operations can affect the amount the dough will rise. In addition, water temperature and oven temperature both affect other variances. On the basis of this information, you should carefully control water and oven temperature and measure the amount dough rises to improve quality.

5. Once you have identified key variances, consider where each variance is observed and controlled as well as what information is needed to control the variance. This information should lead you to ideas for changing the process, information system, roles, and procedures. Ideally, the person closest to the variance should have the ability to control it.

OUTPUT

Now that you have identified possible ways to improve quality or performance, you should evaluate the relative costs and benefits of your options. Assuming

FIGURE 2.9 *Sample Cost/Benefit Analysis*

Options	Install integrated manufacturing computer system	Move storeroom	Implement SPC charts to track quality problems	Eliminate multiple sign-offs on purchase orders
Capital Costs	$15,000	$5,000	—	—
Annual Expenses	5,000	—	$1,000 SPC training $2,000 in work hours	Potential for abuse
Annual Savings	$10,000 (est.)	$2,000 in work hours	$50,000 in reduced waste (est.)	Shorter downtime Faster processing of orders Save managers one hour per week
Return on Investment	3 years payback period	2.5 years payback period	$47,000 net savings per year (est.)	N/A

your ideas do not represent huge investments for your organization, you can do some simple calculations to identify the payback for each option. If any of your ideas represent a significant investment, you should ask a financial analyst to help you do a more sophisticated analysis.

Cost/Benefit Analysis

A sample cost/benefit analysis is shown in Figure 2.9. To complete a cost/benefit analysis, follow these steps:

1. List your most promising options across the top of the chart.

2. For each option, list any related expenses. If you are purchasing something that will have value for more than one year (e.g., equipment or new office furniture) put the purchase price under capital costs. List any annual expenses as well (e.g., lease payments, rent, fees, and training). Then estimate the annual savings the option will bring. If your option will not cost anything, list possible hidden costs and potential benefits.

3. Compute the return on investment for each option. Use this formula if you have capital costs:

$$\text{capital cost}/(\text{annual savings} - \text{annual expenses}) = \text{payback period in years}$$

Use this formula if you do not have capital costs:

annual savings − annual expenses = net savings per year

FOLLOW-UP

Share the information from the diagrams you completed and your cost/benefit analysis with your work group and ask for input. Finalize the information and present it to the steering committee.

Get steering committee feedback on any issues or recommendations that might affect policy or other work groups.

PREPARATION FOR NEXT STEPS

Review Step 3—Conduct Social Analysis—and decide which tools you will use.

3

Conduct Social Analysis

"We live and learn, but not the wiser grow."

—John Pomfret

Now that you have a good understanding of the technical aspects of your work, we need to examine the social or human side. To be most effective, job design must take into account the needs of the people as well as the nature of the work. In this step, we'll examine opportunities for you to improve job satisfaction as well as productivity by changing roles, responsibilities, and group norms.

OVERVIEW

In this step, you must identify possible changes to team membership and roles. You must also identify any important obstacles that must be removed for you to be successful. The purpose of this step is to identify potential changes that should be made to your team membership, structure, or practices that will support teamwork. You will complete up to four types of social analysis:

- A network diagram to help you determine whether all the right players are on the team.
- A responsibility chart to clarify technical job responsibilities and identify opportunities for cross-training or job enrichment.
- A leadership roles diagram to clarify how the leadership roles will be handled on the team.
- A team assessment to identify any significant obstacles to teamwork.

By the end of this step, you should have created:

- Charts for at least three organizational options.
- A listing of practices that are inconsistent with teams.

DECISION CHECKLIST

Using the decision checklist shown in Figure 3.1, identify the most important tools and processes for your design team to perform during this step.

TEAM-BUILDING ACTIVITY—SUPPORTIVE SYSTEMS

Conduct the team-building activity for step 3 (shown in Figure 3.2). Write the question on a flip chart and ask each person to jot down his or her answer. Allow one or two minutes for contemplation. Then ask each person to share his or her answer. After all have shared their answers, summarize the common themes or comments under the question on the flip chart.

TOOLS AND PROCESSES

Network Diagram

The purpose of the network diagram is to help you identify appropriate changes to team membership. For instance, manufacturing teams often require significant support from maintenance and engineering. When these groups have different goals or priorities, it can cause conflict. Often the best solution is to reassign someone from the support functions to the team. This is appropriate only if you need at least one full-time person. If not, you should establish a customer-supplier relationship between the team and the support function.

Teams can be organized in a number of ways, and each way would lead you to make different choices about who should be on the team. You can organize around:

- A whole process.
- A whole product.
- Specific customers.

FIGURE 3.1 *Decision Checklist for Step 3*

✔ = This analysis would be useful
✕ = This analysis may NOT be useful; use another tool

If you have:	Network Diagram	Responsibility Chart	Leadership Roles Diagram	Team Assessment
• Friction with other work groups	✔	✔		
• Friction within your work group		✔	✔	✔
• Suggested changes to the work process that might change the number of people or positions	✔	✔		
• Bad, unpleasant jobs		✔		✔
• Boring jobs	✔	✔	✔	
• Lack of clarity about how leadership roles will be handled		✔	✔	
• Existing habits, norms, or practices that discourage teamwork				✔
• Been told to focus only within your existing work group or already have natural work teams	✕			
• No need for flexibility in staffing or job enrichment		✕		
• Been provided detailed information on how to handle leadership roles			✕	
• Exceptional teamwork now				✕

FIGURE 3.2 *Team-Building Activity for Step 3*

Step	Category	Question	Purpose
3	Supportive systems	Think of an organizational system (e.g., business planning, purchasing, or compensation) that does not support quality and teamwork. How could you see that system being changed?	Provide input into inconsistent practices chart

- A geographic territory.
- Type of work (i.e., by function).
- Time (i.e., as in shifts).

You might want to create a network diagram around several of these options. A sample network diagram is shown in Figure 3.3.

To complete a network diagram, follow these steps:

1. Draw a circle in the center of a flip chart and label it "our team." If people on your team perform very different functions, list the primary team positions within the circle.

2. Draw and label additional circles around "our team" to represent other groups you interact with on a regular basis.

FIGURE 3.3 *Sample Network Diagram*

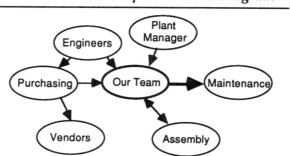

3. Draw arrows between "our team" and the other circles to represent the primary flow of information: from "our team" outward, in toward the team, or both directions.

4. Fatten or highlight the arrows for critical relationships or frequent interactions.

5. On the basis of this information, identify any functions that should be added to (or removed from) the team. If you add someone to the team, you should be able to justify needing at least one full-time person. Draw a revised network diagram (shown in Figure 3.4) representing the changes you are suggesting. You may want to draw a couple different options.

FIGURE 3.4 *Sample Revised Network Diagram*

6. Consider the remaining arrows and decide if any should be added, deleted, or changed. For instance, you may decide that information should go in both directions instead of just one direction. In a different color pen, draw your recommended changes to the arrows and briefly note how the existing communication channels should be changed.

Sometimes it is easier to diagram your network by working from an organization chart or process diagram. Feel free to use a different approach than the bub-

FIGURE 3.5 *Alternative Techniques for Network Diagramming*

Working from an Organization Chart

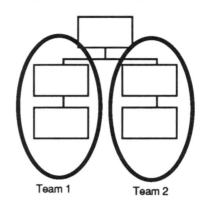

Team 1   Team 2

Working from a Process Diagram

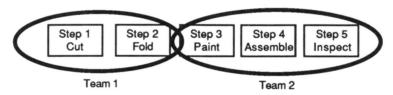

Team 1   Team 2

ble diagram method used in these examples. Figure 3.5 shows some alternative diagramming techniques.

Responsibility Chart

A responsibility chart helps to identify appropriate changes to job definitions and responsibilities that will result in improved job satisfaction and performance. When you complete the chart, be sure to include any additional roles you added from the network diagram or any process changes you identified from your technical analysis in step 2. Figure 3.6 shows a sample responsibility chart for making origami figures.

To complete a responsibility chart, follow these steps:

1. List the main steps in the process across the top of the chart.

2. List the positions and number of people holding each position down the left side of the chart.

FIGURE 3.6 *Sample Responsibility Chart*

Positions	Situations			Process				
	Bad	Boring	Bottleneck	Cut	Crease	Fold	Paint	Assemble
Cutter (2)				Cut paper	Crease 2X			
Folder (2)			✔			Fold 3X		
Painter (2)	✔		✔				Color 1 side	
Assembler (2)		✔						Open 2X
Supervisor (1)								Inspect

3. For each position, check any of the situations that exist now: the three *B*s. Is the position a Bad job (i.e., dirty, uncomfortable, or degrading), a Boring job, or a Bottleneck?

4. Under each step in the process, describe each position's involvement and draw arrows to represent the flow. Use simple action verbs such as write, make, build, check, package, verify, approve, or inspect. Your chart should show how work actually gets completed (or would get completed if you changed the process), not how theoretical procedures or job descriptions claim it gets done.

5. Analyze the chart for the following conditions: wrong people performing the task, not all the right people involved, closely related tasks performed by different people when they might be better done by the same person. Consider how these conditions affect the situations you checked. Discuss possible solutions, including combining jobs, revising job responsibilities, cross-training team members, or rotating responsibilities. For instance, you may decide that all team members should learn how to do regular maintenance on their machines, or that each person should be responsible for cleaning his or her own area so that no one has to be janitor.

6. Redraw the chart incorporating your suggested changes (see Figure 3.7). Try to resolve the negative situations you identified and note how they are improved on the chart. You may want to draw a couple of different options.

Leadership Roles Diagram

Self-directed teams take on most if not all the responsibilities of a traditional supervisor. These leadership roles, defined by a hand-off list, must be delegated to members of the team. It is important to spread these responsibilities among team members to avoid turning a team leader into a traditional supervisor. Your steering committee may have established roles that all teams should have. If so, you can add to their roles if necessary and plan how to adapt the roles to your work.

FIGURE 3.7 *Revised Responsibility Chart*

Positions	Changes	Process				
		Cut	Crease	Fold	Paint	Assemble
Cutter (0)	Eliminate task	Buy cut paper				
Folder (4)	Cross-train cutters			Fold 3X Inspect		
Painter/ Assembler (4)	Combine paint & assembly				Color 1 side	Open 2X Inspect
Supervisor (1)	Change role					Customer liaison

If your steering committee has established leadership roles all teams must have, then work with their information. If the steering committee has not provided any guidance, you have more flexibility in the roles you select and how you diagram their relationships.

There are two common ways to diagram leadership roles. One is to draw a star with a point for every role. Figure 3.8 shows a sample star leadership role diagram. This may be the best approach if your design team is only responsible for redesigning one work group.

FIGURE 3.8 *Sample Leadership Role Diagram—Star*

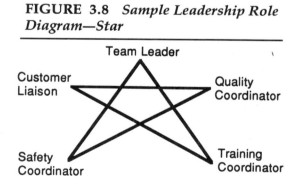

The other approach is to draw ovals to show the interrelationships between teams (see Figure 3.9). This may be more appropriate if your design team is responsible for multiple work teams.

FIGURE 3.9   *Sample Leadership Role Diagram—Ovals*

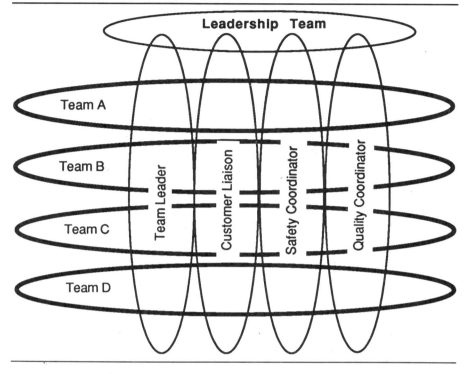

Regardless of the approach you select, follow these steps to complete your leadership role diagram:

1. Write the responsibilities from your hand-off list on small pieces of paper or adhesive-backed notes.

2. If you have been given standard leadership roles, organize the responsibilities under those headings on a flip chart. Include a heading for "All team members." If necessary, identify any new roles. If you have *not* been assigned standard roles, cluster the responsibilities into logical groupings and then label the categories.

3. Draw a visual (like those in Figures 3.8 and 3.9) that shows the leadership roles. Under each role, list the key functions that role will perform (e.g., a team leader may run team meetings, keep meeting minutes, and gather agenda items from other leadership roles). Capture the essence of the role. It is not necessary to list every task that role will perform.

Team Assessment

Many things can prevent teams from operating effectively. Teams need more than an open, trusting environment to succeed. According to research, eight dimensions must be satisfied for effective team operation.[3] These are discussed in the following section.

Shared Goals. Teams need clear, elevating goals. Troubled teams have often let something else be elevated above the goal. Problems include too many goals, lack of focus, and vague missions. A poor showing in this category is a common factor in ineffective teams.

Results-Oriented Structure. Teams need to be organized effectively, providing a results-driven structure. This implies that the right people are on the team and that the roles result in efficient and effective behavior. There are three types of teams, each having its own implications for structure and membership: problem resolution, creative, and tactical teams. Necessary features of team structure include clear roles and accountabilities, effective communication systems, methods to monitor individual performance and provide feedback, and fact-based judgments.

Competent Members. Team members must be competent technically, interpersonally, and in group settings.

Committed Staff. Those on the team must share a unified commitment to the end result. Commitment is fostered through involvement. Unity is based on balancing differentiation and integration (valuing diversity versus requiring conformity and groupthink).

Collaborative Climate. Effective teams exhibit a high degree of openness, trust, and collaboration. Competitiveness within an effective team is minimal.

Standards of Excellence. High-performing teams have high standards of excellence. This implies not only that high standards are set, but also that they are enforced by the team and that the team continuously strives to improve.

---

[3]Larson, Carl E. and LaFasto, Frank MJ (1989). *TeamWork: What Must Go Right/What Can Go Wrong*. Newbury Park, CA: Sage Publications, Inc.

Effective Leadership. Effective teams require competent, principled leadership. Leaders must provide the team adequate autonomy but support the team when it needs help. Leaders should also provide a vision and challenge that inspires the team to excel.

Supportive Systems. Effective teams rest upon a base of supportive systems. These systems should provide for measurements, external support and recognition, and group rewards. You may want to consider which of these systems may need to be changed:

- Strategic and business planning.
- Measurements.
- Reporting.
- Performance appraisal.
- Compensation and rewards.
- Customer and supplier feedback.
- Purchasing.
- Budgeting.
- Financial tracking.
- Production scheduling and work planning.
- Hiring and selection.
- Training.

To identify your obstacles to effective team operation, conduct a team assessment by following these steps:

1. Create force field flip charts for each of the eight dimensions. Write the name of the dimension on the top of the chart. Then create a force field chart underneath. Figure 3.10 shows a partially completed chart.

2. Assign charts to groups of team members and read the description of the dimension. Then brainstorm helping and hindering forces—that is, those things that are working for you and against you.

FIGURE 3.10 *Sample Force Field Chart for Team Assessment*

SHARED GOALS

Helping forces	*Hindering forces*
Report to same vice-president We get regular info on performance	We are measured on different things We have no input into goals

Suggested Actions

- Increase frequency of performance reporting
- Change goal setting process to allow team input
-

3. Identify the strongest helping forces and list ways to strengthen them. List these under "Suggested Actions."

4. Identify the strongest hindering forces and list ways to reduce their impact. List these under "Suggested Actions."

5. Report the results from steps 2 through 4 to the entire team and identify actions that should be taken to support the implementation of teams.

OUTPUT

Now you must summarize the data you have collected during the social analysis. You should diagram your best organizational options and list obstacles and possible solutions.

PMI Chart and Organizational Options

Your network diagrams and responsibility charts should provide you with several organizational options for job responsibilities. Remember that there are many ways to organize a team. For instance, you can organize around:

- A whole process.
- A whole product.
- Specific customers.
- A geographic territory.

- Type of work (i.e., by function).
- Time (i.e., as in shifts).

Pick at least three options that you think are most promising and complete the following steps:

1. Draw the optional structures for job responsibilities (or use an existing network diagram). Draw at least three options.
2. Give each option an identifiable name (e.g., Add Maintenance, or By Product).
3. Under each option, add a PMI chart, listing the Pluses, Minuses, and what's Interesting about each option. Figure 3.11 shows a sample chart. Be sure to

FIGURE 3.11 *Sample PMI Chart*

Add Maintenance

Engineer gives advice on purchases; team orders

Plant Manager gets monthly team reports

Engineers

Plant Manager

Purchasing

Our Team
Maintenance

Organizational change: Assign one maintenance person per shift to team

Vendors

Assembly

Establish way for team to notify vendors of quality problems

Pluses	Minuses	Interesting
Aligns goals of maintenance and production	May make it more difficult to get help if our maintenance technician is on vacation	Might lead to more cross-training where operators do basic maintenance

identify any issues that might affect company policy or other work groups (e.g., changes to human resource systems, job bidding procedures, job descriptions, work schedules, or resource requirements).

4. If you identified more than one set of leadership roles, complete steps 1 through 3 for the leadership roles as well. If you have only one set of leadership roles, you can use the charts you have already completed; simply clean up your existing leadership roles diagram if necessary.

Inconsistent Practices

To summarize your team assessment, list the most pressing obstacles and brainstorm at least three actions that could be taken to mitigate them. A sample inconsistent practices chart is shown in Figure 3.12.

FIGURE 3.12 *Sample Inconsistent Practices Chart*

Category	Obstacle	Possible Actions
Shared goals	Goals of maintenance and production not compatible	• Add maintenance technician to each team • Have maintenance and production report to same manager
Supportive systems	Rewards are for individuals, not teams, which creates competition.	• Implement group-based compensation system • Let teams have input into rewards

FOLLOW-UP

Share your organizational options and inconsistent practices charts with your work group and ask for input. Finalize the information and present the information to the steering committee.

Get steering committee feedback on any issues or recommendations that might affect policy or other work groups.

Share the detailed results of the team assessment with your work group and/ or all those who participated.

PREPARATION FOR NEXT STEPS

Review the next step, combine ideas, and decide which tools you will use.

If you decide to use a weighted criteria chart in step 4, it is helpful to get steering committee input on the criteria and their weights before completing the chart.

4

Combine Ideas

"Every act of creation is first of all an act of destruction."

—Pablo Picasso

So far, you have analyzed the technical and social systems associated with your work. You may have generated ideas for changing the process, technology, or roles. All these ideas are interrelated, however. For instance, if you automate a portion of your process (i.e., a change in technology), you may open new opportunities to change the process or create a need to change the physical layout. You will certainly change some job responsibilities, and how you decide to integrate the technology will affect whether you create more of the three *B*s: bad jobs, boring jobs, or bottlenecks. Now it is time to analyze the interrelationships and select from your ideas the best combination of recommendations so that performance and job satisfaction are optimized.

OVERVIEW

In this step, you must select the best combination of ideas. If no organizational option is clearly preferable, you should complete a weighted criteria chart. At a minimum, you should select one organizational option and list the necessary actions to implement the technical changes you identified in step 2 and overcome the obstacles you identified in step 3.

In this step, you may complete:

- A weighted criteria chart to analyze your options.
- An interrelationship worksheet to identify interrelationships between ideas.

You will prepare a presentation to the steering committee, which includes:

- Recommended team structure.
- Associated changes.

DECISION CHECKLIST

Using the decision checklist shown in Figure 4.1, identify the most important tools and processes for your design team to perform during this step.

FIGURE 4.1 *Decision Checklist for Step 4*

✔ = This analysis would be useful
✗ = This analysis may NOT be useful; use another tool

If you have:	Weighted Criteria Chart	Interrelationship Worksheet
• No organizational option that is clearly better than the others	✔	
• Complex obstacles or recommendations that require multiple actions to implement		✔

TEAM-BUILDING ACTIVITY—COMPETENT MEMBERS

Conduct the next team building activity. Write the question shown in Figure 4.2 on a flip chart and ask each person to jot down his or her answer. Allow

FIGURE 4.2 *Team-Building Activity for Step 4*

Step	Category	Question	Purpose
4	Competent members	What is a skill that you have only used away from work that could be an asset in our new organization?	Reveal the untapped talents of employees

one or two minutes for comtemplation. Then ask each person to share his or her answer. After all have shared their answers, summarize the common themes or comments under the question on the flip chart.

TOOLS AND PROCESSES

Weighted Criteria Chart

The human mind is not set up to evaluate many options at one time. Weighted criteria charts help you deal with multiple variables. You identify and weigh the criteria you want to apply to your options and then compare each option against each criterion. This allows your mind to focus on only one issue at a time.

If it is not clear which organizational option is best, complete a weighted criteria chart like the sample shown in Figure 4.3 by following these steps:

FIGURE 4.3 *Sample Weighted Criteria Chart*

Criteria	Weight	Option 1	Option 2	Option 3	Option 4
Cost	1	10 10	5 5	1 1	7 7
Quality	10	1 10	10 100	8 80	3 30
Customer satisfaction	7	7 49	6 42	10 70	1 7
TOTAL		69	147	151	44

1. List the criteria down the left side of the chart. Include the business reasons for implementing teams (e.g., improving quality or reducing cost) as well as the human or social criteria (e.g., more interesting work, less stress, or improved employee satisfaction).

2. Rate each criterion from 1 to 10 with 10 being the most important and 1 being the least important on the list. It is often easiest to find the 10 and 1 first. Then ask, ''If this is 10 and this is a 1, how would you rate this next criterion?'' Although people may resist using the lower numbers, it is important to spread out your ratings.

3. List your organizational options across the top and rate each option against each criteria using the same 1 through 10 scale. Place these ratings in the small boxes within the matrix. Which option best meets the first criterion? That's a 10. Which option least meets the criterion? That's a 1. How do the other options fall within that range?

4. Multiply each rating by the weight and write the product in the bigger boxes.

5. Add up the products (the numbers in the bigger boxes) for each option. The number with the largest score should be your best option. It's okay to use intuition, too. If the team has a negative initial reaction to the result, reevaluate your weightings and go through the process again.

6. Once you decide on an organizational structure, clean up your organization chart from your social analysis in step 3 if necessary. Be sure it lists how many people should occupy each position.

Interrelationship Worksheet

Every change you make may affect other changes. The interrelationship worksheet helps you to identify these interrelationships. Figure 4.4 shows a sample worksheet.

Follow these steps to complete your own worksheet:

1. List all the changes you are considering down the left side of the worksheet as well as across the top. If desired, you can categorize them by the type of change they represent (i.e., social changes to the structure, roles, norms, and rewards; or technical changes to the process, physical layout, technology, and methods).

2. Then look at each relationship and determine whether the two changes are

FIGURE 4.4 *Sample Interrelationship Worksheet*

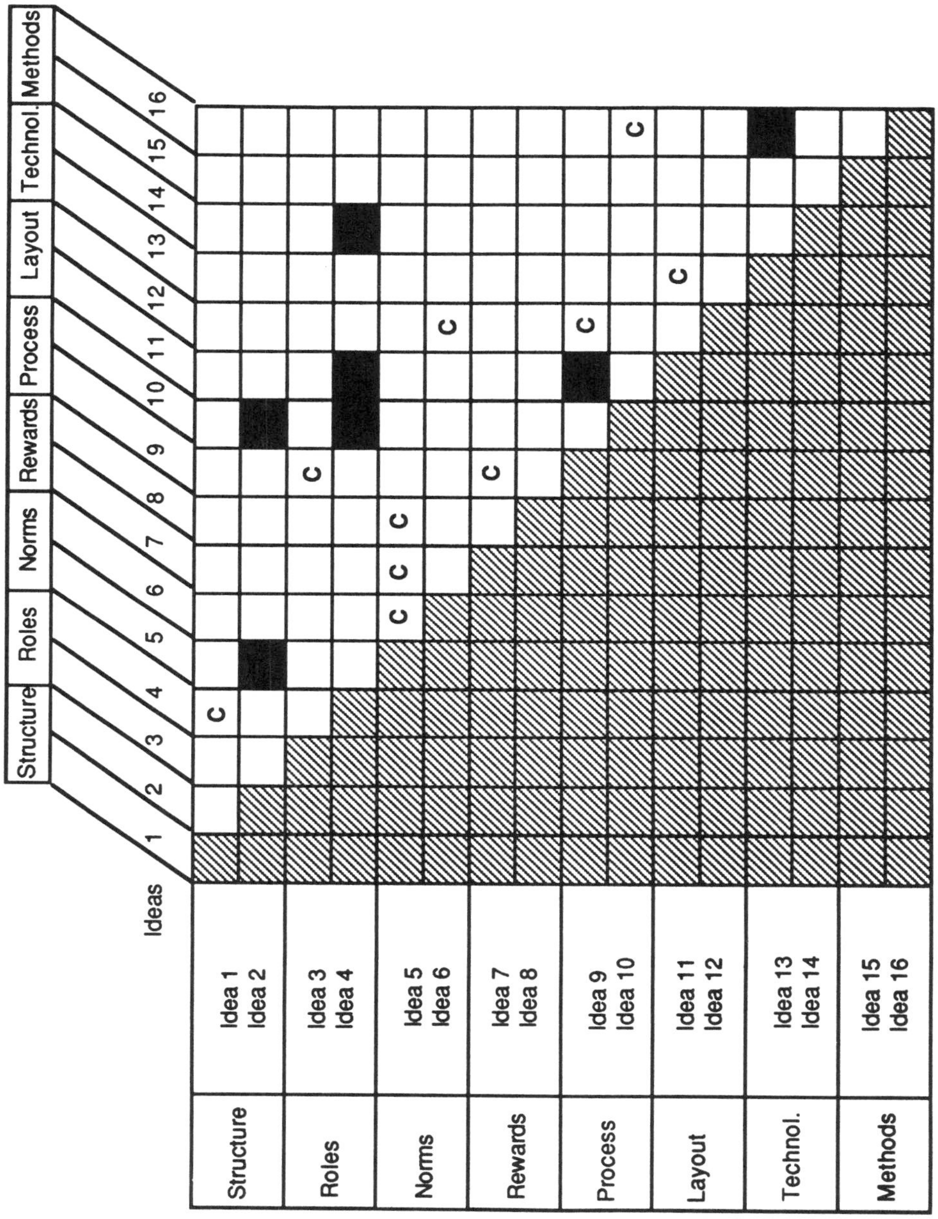

compatible or incompatible. Place a C in the square where they intersect if they are compatible. If they are incompatible, darken the square.

3. Where changes are incompatible, consider creative strategies to make them compatible. If you cannot find a way to make them compatible, decide which change is more important. If some items are only somewhat incompatible, you can darken a triangle instead of the entire square.

OUTPUT

Once you have completed these tasks, you should prepare a presentation for the steering committee. Your presentation should include:

*   The recommended team structure for both job and leadership roles—that is, what you chose and why. You can clean up your weighted criteria and PMI charts for this purpose.

*   A thorough discussion of your recommended associated changes and their cost/benefits. The following section provides the suggested format for presenting these recommendations.

Associated Changes

Next you should document all the related changes and recommendations you are making. These may include ideas from your technical analysis in step 2 (e.g., changes to physical layout, process, technology, or methods) or social analysis in step 3 (i.e., ideas to remove obstacles to teamwork). You can take your ideas off the interrelationships worksheet if you completed one.

To document your recommendations, complete an associated changes sheet (see Figure 4.5) by following these steps:

1. For each problem or opportunity you identified, list your recommendations as either ''Need to have'' or ''Nice to have.''

2. Note the associated costs and benefits for each recommendations. You can use a minus sign before costs and a plus sign before benefits.

FIGURE 4.5 *Sample Associated Changes Sheet*

Problem or Opportunity	*Need to Have*	*Cost/Benefit*	*Nice to Have*	*Cost/Benefit*
Can eliminate 3 steps in process with a change in technology	Computer system	−$5000 +Savings of 2,000 work hours per year		
Compensation system does not reward teamwork	Group-based variable compensation system	−Increase labor costs +Might not add to base pay +Should result in higher performance	Pay for skills system	−Tends to increase salary costs −Can be complex to administer +Would encourage cross-training, which leads to more flexibility

It's a good idea to complete a dry run of your presentation to identify tough questions and issues the steering committee might raise.

FOLLOW-UP

Give your presentation to your work group and get their commitment to support the recommendations. If appropriate, ask for input from such other key groups as human resources, union leaders, and the like.

Present your recommendations to the steering committee and secure their approval.

PREPARATION FOR NEXT STEPS

Review step 5, Formalize Recommendations, and decide which tools you will use.

Gather any necessary policies or forms that are relevant to job descriptions, cross-training, or the selection and bidding process. For instance, your organization may have a standard format for job descriptions, the training department may have a catalog of available courses, or bidding for jobs may be bound by union contracts.

5

Formalize Recommendations

"The palest ink is better than the best memory."

—Chinese proverb

By now, you should have a clear understanding of the recommendations the steering committee accepted. Now it is time to make those general recommendations more specific. You'll need to add detail to roles, training needs, and plans.

OVERVIEW

In this step, you will formalize roles, training requirements, and selection processes as well as lay out an implementation timetable. Depending on your needs, you may complete:

- Sign-up sheets for any teams whose roles or members have changed.
- A responsibility matrix to clarify responsibilities for highly interdependent positions.
- Leadership roles worksheets to clarify the responsibilities of each leadership role.
- A training plan that specifies the training necessary for specific positions, cross-training, and the team as a whole.

You should also:

- Draft an implementation timetable.
- Modify any job descriptions for any positions that have changed.

DECISION CHECKLIST

Using the decision checklist shown in Figure 5.1, identify the most important tools and processes for your design team to perform during this step.

TEAM-BUILDING ACTIVITY—COLLABORATIVE CLIMATE

Conduct the team-building activity shown in Figure 5.2. Write the question on a flip chart and ask each person to jot down his or her answer. Allow one or two minutes for contemplation. Then ask each person to share his or her answers. After all have shared their answers, summarize the common themes or comments under the question on the flip chart.

TOOLS AND PROCESSES

Sign-Up Sheet

Often, a design team is creating a team structure for more than one team or the reorganization results in changes to roles and responsibilities. When this occurs, you need a way to decide who is going to do what. Although you can have managers assign people, it is usually preferable to let people sign up for the team and positions they want. You will need a sign-up sheet to help facilitate this process (see Figure 5.3). However, if the positions are significantly different than what the team members have been doing or if pay rates will change, you should not use a sign-up sheet. Instead, implement your normal job-bidding process.

Follow these steps to complete a sign-up sheet:

1. For each team, list the positions down the left side and indicate the number of people needed in those positions.

2. On the right side, draw lines for people to sign up. For instance if you need three operators on team A, draw three lines.

FIGURE 5.1 *Decision Checklist for Step 5*

✔ = This analysis would be useful
✗ = This analysis may NOT be useful; use another tool

If you have:	Sign-Up Sheet	Responsibility Matrix	Leadership Roles Worksheet	Training Plan
• A need to assign people to positions	✔			
• Highly interdependent positions		✔		
• Had role confusion or trouble coordinating the roles in the past		✔		
• A lack of clarity around how leadership roles will be handled			✔	
• Changed position descriptions significantly	✗			
• Been provided detailed information on how to handle leadership roles			✗	
• Planned to cross-train team members				✔
• Leadership responsibilities that team members don't know how to perform				✔
• A thorough training needs analysis already completed				✗

FIGURE 5.2 *Team-Building Activity for Step 5*

Step	Category	Question	Purpose
5	Collaborative climate	Think of an interaction that actually occurred in this team or organization and that you think should be handled differently in the future. How did the interaction violate the values you identified in step 1 and how should similar situations be handled in the future?	Reveal additional training or support needed to implement a team-based culture

FIGURE 5.3 *Sample Sign-Up Sheet*

TEAM: _____

POSITIONS	NUMBER	TEAM MEMBERS
Folders	4	_____
		_____
		_____
		_____
Painter/Assembler	4	_____
		_____
		_____
		_____
Maintenance	1	_____

3. When the time comes to set up teams, you can post these sign-up sheets and give team members a deadline to pick a team. Consider how you will resolve the following possible situations:

- No one is signing up.

- More than one person wants a specific position.

- The resulting team is missing key competencies.

Responsibility Matrix

Some teams are highly interdependent. When it is not clear who is responsible for a task or who should be consulted, problems occur. A responsibility matrix like the one shown in Figure 5.4 helps formalize these relationships.

FIGURE 5.4 *Sample Responsibility Matrix*

Task/Positions	Architect	Builder	Client
Determine needs	C	I	R
Draw up blueprints	R	C	C, A
Estimate building costs	I	R	A
Procure financing		I	R
Subcontract work as necessary		R	I
Construct building	C	R	A
Secure all permits		R	

To build a responsibility matrix, follow these steps:

1. List the tasks or steps in the process (or the deliberations for nonrepetitive processes) down the left side of the diagram.

2. List all the involved parties (members of the network) across the top.

3. Then indicate the degree to which each person should be involved using these codes: R = responsible; C = consulted; I = informed; and A = approves.

4. Analyze the diagram. Make sure that only one person or group is responsible for a task (at any one time) and that the most appropriate party has been selected. Eliminate any unnecessary approvals. Ensure that all the affected parties are consulted or informed as appropriate.

Leadership Roles Worksheet

In step 3, social analysis, you identified the leadership roles you wanted to have in your team. Now you must formalize what those individuals will do and how they will be selected. To do this, complete a leadership roles worksheet for each position. Figure 5.5 shows a sample worksheet; complete your own by following these steps:

FIGURE 5.5 *Sample Leadership Roles Worksheet*

LEADERSHIP ROLE: Quality Coordinator

Tasks	Frequency	Standards
• Process run chart	Daily	Use SPC methods; complete on all four steps in process
• Customer survey	Two times per year	Use existing customer survey form
• Analyze results of quality experiments	As needed	Use standard design-of-experiments methods

ROLE REQUIREMENTS

Must have basic math skills and knowledge of statistical computer software. Must complete the following training or demonstrate equivalent knowledge:

• Basic algebra.
• Quality tools and techniques workshop.
• Advanced statistical process control seminar.
• Introductory seminar on statistical software we will use.

SELECTION PROCEDURE

Rotation will be once every six months. The understudy will move into role and a new understudy will be selected. The understudy will be chosen from a pool of applicants expressing interest in the role, giving preference to those who have not yet held the role. During the six-month understudy period, the understudy will take any of the necessary training based on recommendations from the area manager as well as the retiring and new quality coordinators.

1. List the name of the role and describe its main purpose.

2. List the tasks the role should perform, the frequency of those tasks, and any important standards by which they should perform the tasks. Be as specific as necessary to guide a new person in the role.

3. List the requirements for the role. What knowledge, skills, training, or experience must someone have to fulfill the role? Specify any certification, training, or apprenticeship programs you feel would be necessary to prepare team members for the role.

4. Describe your selection procedure. Be consistent with any guidelines your steering committee has provided you. Provide answers to these questions: How often will you rotate people through the position (daily, weekly, monthly, or semi-annually; three to six months is common)? How will you select that person (vote, nominate, certify, or use understudies)? Must everyone rotate through the position or only those who are interested or who qualify?

Training Plan

Self-directed work teams require a substantial amount of training to be effective. It is therefore necessary to identify who needs what training by completing a training plan (see Figure 5.6). The following steps should be taken to develop a training plan.

1. List all positions and roles across the top of the plan.

2. List the topics or training classes along the left side of the diagram. Remember to include team skills as well as technical job skills.

3. Identify the key content each class should provide.

4. Indicate who should attend each class or topic. If order of the training is important, you can indicate the order in which classes should be taken by numbers.

OUTPUT

Job Descriptions

If you have created any new positions or significantly changed any responsibilities, identify the necessary changes to job descriptions.

FIGURE 5.6 *Sample Training Plan*

Topic or Class	Content	Whole Team	Folders	Painter	Team Leader	Quality Coordinator	Safety Coordinator
Team charter	Mission, goals, key result areas	✓					
Team building	Team roles, problems, communications skills	✓					
Paint mixing	Types of paint, colors			1			
Paint safety	Regulations, hazards, equipment			2			✓
Running meetings	Agendas, preparation, controlling dicsussion, meeting roles				✓	✓	✓

Implementation Timetable

You should begin drafting an implementation plan that shows what will be done to get the teams up and running and by when. A sample implementation timetable is shown in Figure 5.7. Focus on those tasks that must be completed before the teams begin operation and tasks that should be completed within the first three to six months afterward. Your timetable should include the following items:

- When final team structures will be announced.
- When teams will be selected (and sign-up sheets completed).
- When teams will begin operation.
- When early training sessions will be conducted.
- When each leadership role will be filled (you may want to phase them in one at a time).
- Which early hand-offs are to be delegated to the team.
- How and when to communicate these changes with associated work groups, vendors, and customers.
- Costs associated with any of the tasks.

FIGURE 5.7 *Sample Implementation Timetable*

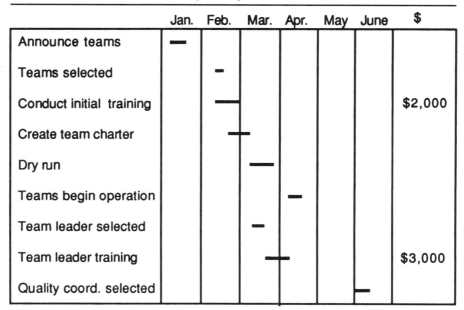

	Jan.	Feb.	Mar.	Apr.	May	June	$
Announce teams	—						
Teams selected		—					
Conduct initial training		—					$2,000
Create team charter			—				
Dry run			—				
Teams begin operation				—			
Team leader selected			—				
Team leader training				—			$3,000
Quality coord. selected						—	

FOLLOW-UP

Present the results of your formalized recommendations and timetable to your teams and the steering committee.

If job descriptions need to be updated, coordinate the changes with your human resources department. If you have created a new position or if job functions have changed significantly, you may also need to conduct a compensation study.

PREPARATION FOR NEXT STEPS

Review step 6, formalize related changes, and decide which tools you will use.

Gather information that will help you make decisions about technical process changes (e.g., equipment specifications and price lists or bids on construction projects) as well as information about alternative human resource and business systems.

6

Formalize Related Changes

"Genius is one percent inspiration and ninety-nine percent perspiration."
—Thomas Edison

Roles and responsibilities are well defined at this time. Now you need to address related changes you have recommended. These may include changes to the process, physical layout, or technology or may involve changes to business systems. These changes all usually involve approvals from those outside the team.

OVERVIEW

In this step, you will finalize plans for technical changes and formalize recommendations that involve other work groups. You should complete this process for any approved recommendations that came out of Step 4, Combining Ideas, unless they were covered in Step 5, Formalize Recommendations.

For each recommendation, you should consider and weigh alternatives, develop a proposal, and build an action plan. Tools you might find useful are:

- Weighted criteria chart.
- PMI chart.
- Cost/benefit analysis.

Because these were covered in previous steps, we will not duplicate the instructions. Please refer to the appropriate sections of this handbook. All tools are listed in the index at the back of the handbook.

FIGURE 6.1 *Decision Checklist for Step 6*

✔ = This analysis would be useful
✕ = This analysis may NOT be useful; use another tool

If you have:	Weighted Criteria Chart	PMI Chart (Plus/Minus/ Interesting)	Cost/Benefit Analysis
• Many options and criteria	✔		
• A few options that differ significantly in nature and approach		✔	
• Options that differ significantly in costs or payment options			✔

DECISION CHECKLIST

Return to the associated changes you presented to the steering committee after step 4. For all those recommendations that were approved, gather information on your options and their respective benefits.

Using the decision checklist shown in Figure 6.1, identify the most important tools and processes for your design team to perform during this step.

TEAM-BUILDING ACTIVITY—STRUCTURE

Conduct the team-building activity shown in Figure 6.2. Write the question on a flip chart and ask each person to jot down his or her answer. Allow one or

FIGURE 6.2 *Team-Building Activity for Step 6*

Step	Category	Question	Purpose
6	Results-oriented structure	If you could spend a week working with someone, following him or her around, who would that be and why?	Reveal needs for information channels, learning opportunities, and changes to structure

two minutes for contemplation. Then ask each person to share his or her answer. After all have shared their answers, summarize the common themes or comments under the question on the flip chart.

TOOLS AND PROCESSES

Weighted Criteria Chart

See Step 4, Combining Ideas.

PMI Chart

See Step 4, Combining Ideas.

Cost/Benefit Analysis

See Step 2, Technical Analysis.

OUTPUT

As a result of this step, you should develop written proposals for all recommendations, being as specific as possible. For instance, if you are changing technology, your proposal should include models or brands of equipment, vendor selected, associated training costs, expected delivery date, and payback period.

Proposal Worksheet

A proposal worksheet like that shown in Figure 6.3 may help you build a convincing proposal. Follow these steps to complete one:

1. State clearly and specifically what you want.

2. Identify the decision maker (i.e., the person or group who has the authority to give you what you want) and any influencers (i.e., people who could influence the decision such as financial analysts or technical experts).

3. Describe the goals of the decision maker and influencers and itemize what each would like and dislike about your proposal.

4. Consider the best way to deliver the proposal. Who should present the idea? Should anyone else be present? When and where should the presentation be made? What information should be included?

FIGURE 6.3 *Sample Proposal Worksheet*

WHAT WE WANT:
HZX Analyzer, Model 4. $40,000 purchase price. $2,000 annual maintenance. Want to send two people to training ($2,000).

DECISION MAKER: Pat McLatimore, Plant Manager

GOALS	*LIKES RE: PROPOSAL*	*DISLIKES RE: PROPOSAL*
Improve quality	HZX would eliminate source of common quality problem	
Reduce costs	Reduce waste	Capital cost and on-going maintenance

INFLUENCERS: Dana Smith, engineer and Danny Vu, team leader

GOALS	*LIKES RE: PROPOSAL*	*DISLIKES RE: PROPOSAL*
Reduce process time	HZX would eliminate one step in process	Could eliminate one position
Reduce changeover time	Once programmed, HZX would speed changeover	Time required to program and de-bug HZX.

BEST WAY TO DELIVER PROPOSAL:
Involve Dana and Danny in reviewing technical options. Prepare thorough cost/benefit analysis for Pat to show payback in less than three years. Do joint presentation to Pat with Dana and Danny.

WE CAN MITIGATE DISLIKES BY:
- Identifying how extra position could be redeployed.
- Getting help from MIS department to program HZX.

FALL-BACK POSITION:
1) Lease HZX 4 with option to buy.
2) HZX Model 2 used equipment available through dealer ($25,000).

5. Consider how to handle the likely objections decision makers and influencers may have.

6. Identify at least one fall-back position, something you can ask for that could give you some of what you want in case the answer to your initial proposal is no.

Action Plan

Some of your proposals will require more than just approval to purchase the item. Some proposals may require the involvement and commitment of other groups within your organization. Develop action plans to negotiate the changes you seek, following the sample shown in Figure 6.4.

FOLLOW-UP

Review your proposals and action plans with your teams and the steering committee. Adjust them as necessary.

FIGURE 6.4 *Sample Action Plan*

Goal: To implement a team-based compensation program that encourages teamwork and optimizes organizational performance without adding to base salaries.

Steps	Person Responsible	Due Date	Completed ✓
1. Research options	Dana	June 5	✓
2. Discuss needs with compensation department	Dana	June 10	
3. Develop draft compensation plan	Compensation Dept.	July 1	
4. Review plan with teams and steering committee	Design Team	July 5	
5. Approval for new compensation plan	Steering Committee	Aug. 1	
6. Implement new compensation system	Compensation Dept.	Jan. 1	

Add relevant tasks from your accepted proposals and action plans to your implementation timetable, which you began in Step 5, Formalize Recommendations.

PREPARATION FOR NEXT STEPS

Review the information associated with Step 7, Troubleshoot the Plan, and decide the best way to conduct a dry run.

Decide who you will invite to the dry run, extend invitations, and schedule the time and location. Ask participants to generate a list of unanswered questions or tough situations that you can use as the basis of the dry run.

7

Troubleshoot the Plan

"To be still searching what we know not by what we know, still closing up truth to truth as we know it . . ."

—John Milton

Before the teams actually begin operation, you should troubleshoot your plan—poke holes in it, try to find the flaws. You want to minimize the confusion and disruption the reorganization will create.

OVERVIEW

In this step, you should brainstorm as many questions and situations as possible and then see if you have a way within your team structure and plan to deal with those situations. You should consider the mundane as well as extraordinary situations.

You might want to conduct a walk-through of a typical day and simulate crises. Involving team members, key customers, and vendors will serve as an effective way of clarifying misconceptions.

Keep track of all the problems you encounter and use that information to strengthen your plan.

TEAM-BUILDING ACTIVITY—COMMITTED STAFF

Conduct the team building activity shown in Figure 7.1. Write the question on a flip chart and ask each person to jot down his or her answer. Allow one or two minutes for contemplation. Then ask each person to share his or her answer. After all have shared their answers, summarize the common themes or comments under the question on the flip chart.

FIGURE 7.1 *Team-Building Activity for Step 7*

Step	Category	Question	Purpose
7	Committed staff	In your new team organization, if you were able to hire the next executive, what characteristics would you look for in the applicants?	Glimpse the far-reaching effects of this organizational change

TOOLS AND PROCESSES

Dry Run Simulation

1. Brainstorm all possible questions and what-if scenarios. Have participants complete the statements:

    • I am concerned that . . .

    • What if . . . happens

    • My worst fear is . . .

2. Cluster the responses into logical categories and eliminate duplicates. Then divide the responses within each category into everyday occurences and special situations.

3. Respond to any issues for which there are already answers.

4. Conduct a walk-through of a typical day and have participants raise issues from their everyday occurrences. Keep track of any issues or problems. Don't try to solve them yet. Keep moving.

5. Decide how the everyday problems should be resolved. Document your agreements.

6. Conduct a second walk-through, applying the resolutions from the previous step. This time, have participants raise special situations. Keep track of any issues or problems. Don't try to solve them yet. Keep moving.

7. Decide how the special situation problems should be resolved. Document your agreements.

8. Discuss any unanswered issues.

OUTPUT

Solutions to the problems encountered during the dry run should be embedded into the plan as appropriate.

FOLLOW-UP

Share the results of your dry run with the steering committee.

PREPARATION FOR NEXT STEPS

Review the information associated with Step 8, Develop a Detailed Implementation Plan.

8

Develop a Detailed Implementation Plan

"The wind of change is blowing . . . "

—Harold MacMillan

Congratulations! You are almost done! Just take one last look at your implementation timetable. In this step, you should focus on what must still be completed before the teams begin operation and what should be done in the first day and month to support their implementation.

OVERVIEW

In this step, you will review and enhance your implementation timetable to make sure all the necessary actions are planned. In particular, you will review a checklist of items that should be addressed. You will add to your timetable as necessary. Your output should include an updated timetable as well as a communication plan.

DECISION CHECKLIST

Using the decision checklist shown in Figure 8.1, identify the most important tools and processes for your design team to perform during this step.

TEAM-BUILDING ACTIVITY—EFFECTIVE LEADERSHIP

Conduct the team-building activity shown in Figure 8.2. Write the question on a flip chart and ask each person to jot down his or her answer. Allow one or

FIGURE 8.1 *Decision Checklist for Step 8*

✔ = This analysis would be useful
✗ = This analysis may NOT be useful; use another tool

If you have:	*Implementation Checklist*	*Communication Plan*
• Not established a detailed plan for the few weeks before and after beginning operation	✔	
• A number of groups that should be informed about your plans.		✔

two minutes for contemplation. Then ask each person to share his or her answer. After all have shared their answers, summarize the common themes or comments under the question on the flip chart.

TOOLS AND PROCESSES

Implementation Checklist

You should have answers to the questions shown in the implementation checklist shown in Figure 8.3. If not, add appropriate tasks to your timetable.

Communication Plan

Different groups may need different types of information. However, if you organize your thoughts, you may be able to build a flexible communication pro-

FIGURE 8.2 *Team-Building Activity for Step 8*

Step	*Category*	*Question*	*Purpose*
8	Effective leadership	If you could ask one person in the organization to do one thing to demonstrate commitment to this change, who would you ask and what would you ask him/her to do?	Generate ideas for communication plan

FIGURE 8.3 *Implementation Checklist*

The First Steps and Immediate Needs

- When will the new teams begin operation?

- How will teams be supported and problems resolved during the first few weeks of operation?

- Which leadership roles will be assigned at the outset, and who will fill those roles?

- Which hand-offs will the teams be responsible for at the outset, and how will they get the necessary training or coaching?

- Who else needs to know about the new teams (e.g., other work groups, customers, or suppliers), and how will you communicate with them?

- What training should the team receive before beginning operating, and how will they find the time to attend the training?

- During implementation, productivity sometimes drops. What flexibility or constraints do the teams have?

- What help is the team likely to need from management in the first few weeks, and how can management get ready to provide that assistance?

Positioning the Team for the Long-Term

- How will the teams develop shared visions and goals?

- How will the teams establish and track their performance?

- What training should the team receive soon after "going live" and how will they find the time to attend the training?

- How will the teams link to their customers and suppliers (internal and/or external)?

- What types of meetings should the team hold and how frequently should they meet for each type of meeting?

- How will teams find time to meet? Will overtime be possible and if so, how much? What are the constraints the team must operate within?

cess that allows you to add or delete segments of information while still providing a consistent message. A communication plan can help you clarify the needs of each audience as well as the best media to use. (For instance, in the example shown in Figure 8.4, we have recommended a video be used to cover the information all groups should receive to make sure all get the same information while the variable content is handled through handouts and discussions.)

FIGURE 8.4 *Sample Communication Plan*

Content	Mgrs.	Staff Groups	Customers	Suppliers	All Employees	Best Media
Why going to self-directed teams	✔	✔	✔	✔	✔	Video
Pilot groups	✔	✔	✔	✔	✔	Video
Start date	✔	✔	✔	✔	✔	Video
Timetable— Details	✔	✔			✔	Handout/ Presentation
Impact on them	✔	✔	✔	✔	✔	Discussion
How we will stay in touch	✔	✔	✔	✔	✔	Discussion
Presenter	Plant Mgr.	Plant Mgr.	Team Leader	Team Leader	Vice-President	

OUTPUT

By the end of this step, you should have a thorough implementation plan as well as a detailed plan for communicating with affected parties.

FOLLOW-UP

If you have chosen any complicated or expensive media (such as video or slides) estimate the cost of producing them.

Share the detailed plan and communication plan with your teams and the steering committee. Get commitment to carry out all steps and responsibilities.

PREPARATION FOR NEXT STEPS

Prepare all related media to carry out your communication plan and implement the communication process.

Implement the tasks on your implementation timetable.

Appendix

RECOMMENDED READING

Block, Peter (1993). *Stewardship: Choosing Service over Self-Interest.* San Francisco: Berrett-Koehler.

> Excellent book on the philosophy and beliefs that self-direction supports.

Bridges, William (1988). *Surviving Corporate Transition: Rational Management in a World of Mergers, Start-Ups, Takeovers, Layoffs, Divestitures, Deregulation, and New Technologies.* Mill Valley, CA: William Bridges and Associates.

> Good book on managing change and transition.

Bureau of National Affairs (1988). ''Changing Pay Practices: New Developments in Employee Compensation.'' Washington DC: BNA *Labor Relations Week* Vol 2, No 24 June 15, 1988.

> Good overview of compensation options. Chapters include monetary and non-monetary rewards as well as case studies from union and non-union settings.

Doyle, Robert (1983). *Gainsharing and Productivity: A Guide to Planning, Implementation, and Development.* New York, NY: American Management Association.

> Helpful step-by-step manual for assessing readiness for and implementing a gainsharing program.

Francis, Dave and Young, Don (1979). *Improving Work Groups: A Practical Manual for Team Building.* San Diego: University Associates.

> Includes many team building activities.

Hammer, Michael (Jul./Aug. 1990). "Reengineering Work: Don't Automate, Obliterate." *Harvard Business Review*, pp. 104–112.

> Includes excellent examples of how process management and work redesign can dramatically improve productivity.

Hanna, David (1988). *Designing Organizations for High Productivity*. New York: Addison Wesley.

> Helpful background reading providing some of the philosophical underpinnings.

Hitchcock, Darcy (December 1992). "Overcoming the Top 10 Self-Directed Team Stoppers." *Journal for Quality and Participation: Association for Quality and Participation*, pp. 42–47.

> Identifies common obstacles to implementing self-directed teams and provides practical suggestions for overcoming them.

Hitchcock, Darcy (Jul/Aug 1994). "When Rafting the SMT River, Think of Your Design Team as a Tour Guide." *Journal for Quality and Participation: Association for Quality and Participation*.

> This forthcoming article explains four common problems design teams encounter and how to overcome them.

Hitchcock, Darcy and Lord, Linda (June 1992). "A Convert's Primer to Socio-Tech." *Journal for Quality and Participation: Association for Quality and Participation*, pp. 46–57.

> Good overview of socio-technical systems design principles, practices, and prophets in lay language.

Klein, Janice (Sept./Oct. 1984). "Why Supervisors Resist Employee Involvement." *Harvard Business Review*, pp. 87–95.

> Provides a way to understand supervisory fears and issues associated with employee involvement efforts.

Larson, Carl E. and LaFasto, Frank MJ (1989). *TeamWork: What Must Go Right/ What Can Go Wrong.* Newbury Park, CA: Sage Publications, Inc.

Good source of data on what makes an effective (generic) team.

Lawler, Edward (1986). *High Involvement Management.* San Francisco: Jossey Bass.

Good source of the history of employee involvement practices (including self-directed work teams) and their demonstrated benefits. Includes many organizational examples and data.

Lawler, Edward III (1990). *Strategic Pay: Aligning Organizational Strategies and Pay Systems.* San Francisco, CA: Jossey Bass.

Amazingly neutral on involvement, Lawler does a remarkable job explaining how to align compensation and performance appraisal to strategic needs.

Orsburn, Moran and Musselwhite, Zenger (1990). *Self-Directed Work Teams: The New American Challenge.* Homewood, IL: Business One Irwin.

Excellent primer on self-directed teams, the implementation process, and related issues.

Pasmore, WA (1988). *Designing Effective Organizations: The Sociotechnical Systems Perspective.* New York, NY: Wiley.

Excellent book providing covering the techniques associated with sociotechnical systems and self-directed teams.

Stayer, Ralph (Nov./Dec. 1990). "How I learned to let my workers lead." *Harvard Business Review*, pp. 66–83.

The Johnsonville Sausage story of how the head of the company learned to let go.

Walton RE (March/April 1985). ''From Control to Commitment in the Workplace.'' *Harvard Business Review*, pp. 77–84.

Good article on benefits and dangers in high-commitment workplaces including diagram comparing three work force strategies: control, transitional, and commitment.

Weisbord, Marvin (1987). Productive Workplaces: Organizing and Managing for Dignity, Meaning, and Community. San Francisco: Jossey Bass.

Good book on managing change.

BLANK WORKSHEETS

DESIGN TEAM CHARTER

Design Team Name:

MISSION:

INDICATORS OF SUCCESS:

KEY RESULT AREAS:
Research and Development:

Sales and Marketing:

Production or Core Work:

Administration:

DESIGN TEAM PLAN

Step	Tasks	Time
1. Get Ready	• Design team charter • Meeting ground rules • Design team plan	
2. Conduct Technical Analysis	• Process diagram • Work flow diagram • Deliberations analysis • Variance matrix • Cost/benefit analysis	
3. Conduct Social Analysis	• Network diagram • Responsibility chart • Leadership roles diagram • Team assessment • PMI chart and organizational options • Inconsistent practices	
4. Combine Ideas	• Weighted criteria chart • Interrelationship worksheet • Associated changes	
5. Formalize Recommendations	• Sign-up sheets • Responsibility matrix • Leadership roles worksheet • Training Plan • Implementation timetable	

(continued)

Step	*Tasks*	*Time*
6. Formalize Related Changes	• Weighted criteria chart • PMI chart • Cost/benefit analysis • Proposal worksheet • Action plan	
7. Troubleshoot the Plan	• Dry run simulation • Solutions to identified problems added to plan	
8. Develop a Detailed Implementation Plan	• Implementation checklist • Communication plan • Completed implementation plan	

PROCESS DIAGRAM (Version 1)

Major Process Step	*Time*

PROCESS DIAGRAM (Version 2)

Person Responsible	*Time*

DELIBERATIONS ANALYSIS

Deliberation	Players: Needs & Brings	Obstacles	Recommendations

VARIANCE MATRIX

Steps   **Key variances**

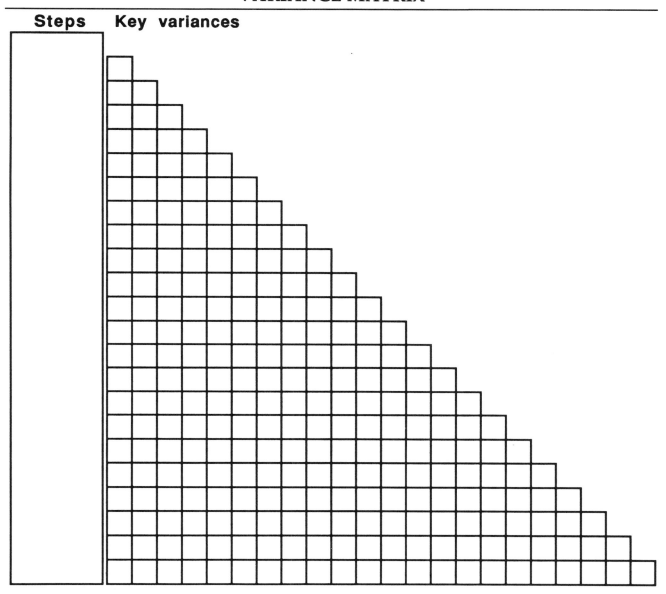

COST/BENEFIT ANALYSIS

Options					
Capital Costs					
Annual Expenses					
Annual Savings					
Return on Investment					

NETWORK DIAGRAM

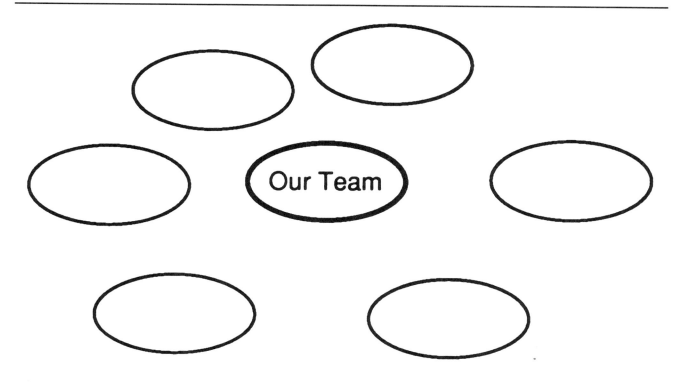

RESPONSIBILITY CHART

CURRENT PROCESS

Positions	Situations			Process
	Bad	Boring	Bottleneck	

REVISED PROCESS

Positions	Changes	Process

LEADERSHIP ROLE DIAGRAMS

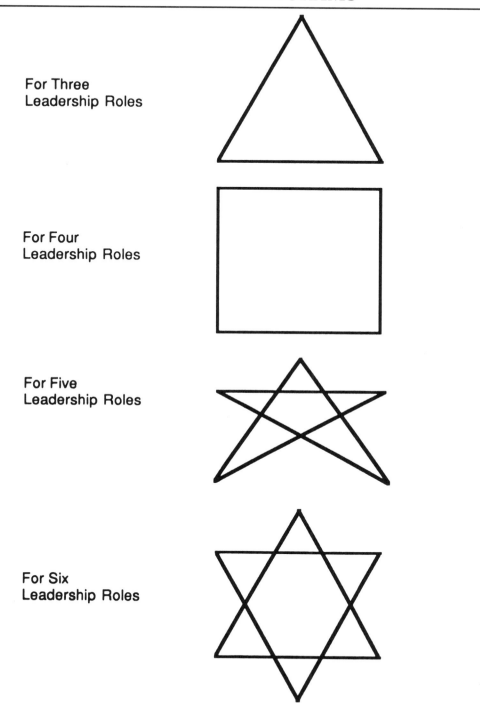

For Three
Leadership Roles

For Four
Leadership Roles

For Five
Leadership Roles

For Six
Leadership Roles

FORCE FIELD (FOR TEAM ASSESSMENT)

DESIRED OUTCOME

Helping forces	*Hindering forces*

Suggested Actions

PMI CHART

Pluses	Minuses	Interesting

INCONSISTENT PRACTICES

Category	Obstacle	Possible Actions

WEIGHTED CRITERIA CHART

Criteria	Weight	Options							
TOTAL									

INTERRELATIONSHIPS WORKSHEET

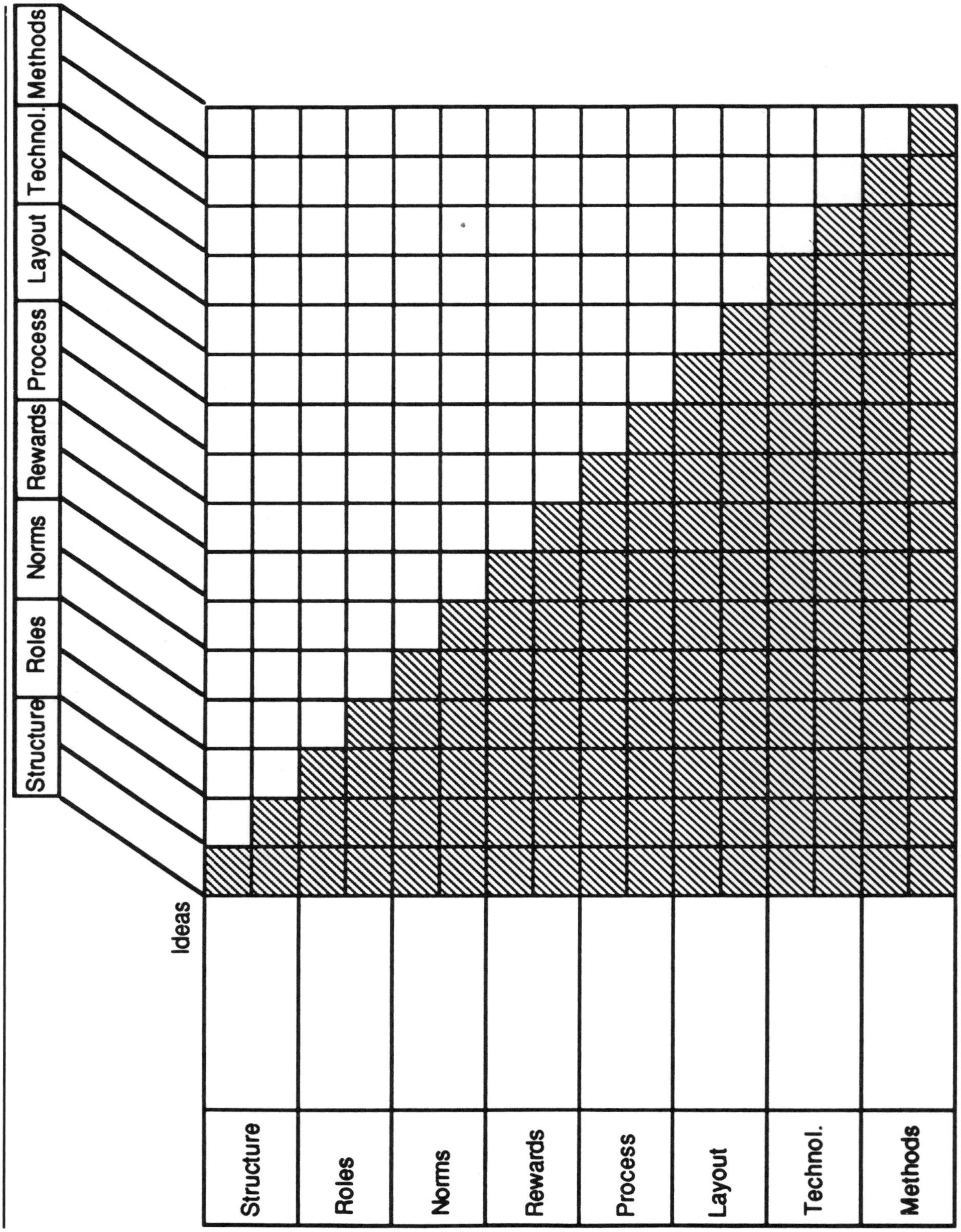
Structure
Roles
Norms
Rewards
Process
Layout
Technol.
Methods
Ideas
Structure
Roles
Norms
Rewards
Process
Layout
Technol.
Methods

ASSOCIATED CHANGES

Problem or Opportunity	Need to Have	Cost/Benefit	Nice to Have	Cost/Benefit

SIGN UP SHEET

TEAM: _____

POSITIONS   **NUMBER**   **TEAM MEMBERS**

RESPONSIBILITIES MATRIX

Task/Positions					

LEADERSHIP ROLES WORKSHEET

LEADERSHIP ROLE:

Tasks	Frequency	Standards

ROLE REQUIREMENTS

SELECTION PROCEDURE

TRAINING PLAN

Topic/Class	Content	Whole Team					

IMPLEMENTATION TIMETABLE

Steps	Time	$

PROPOSAL WORKSHEET

WHAT WE WANT:

DECISION MAKER:

GOALS	*LIKES RE: PROPOSAL*	*DISLIKES RE: PROPOSAL*

INFLUENCERS:

GOALS	*LIKES RE: PROPOSAL*	*DISLIKES RE: PROPOSAL*

BEST WAY TO DELIVER PROPOSAL:

WE CAN MITIGATE DISLIKES BY:

FALL-BACK POSITION:

ACTION PLAN

Goal:

Steps	Person Responsible	Due Date	Completed ✓

COMMUNICATION PLAN

Content	Mgrs.						All Employees	Best Media
Presenter								

Index

Action plan, 61–62, 100
Associated changes, 40, 44–45, 93

Changes, 57–62
  decision checklist, 58
  team building, 58–59
  tools and processes, 59
  see also Associated changes
Collaborative climate, 32, 48, 50
Committed staff, 4, 32, 63–64
Communication plan, 68, 70, 101
Competent members, 3, 32, 40–41
Cost/benefit analysis, 21–22, 57, 84

Deliberations analysis, 12, 17–18, 19, 82
Design team charter, 4–7, 77
Design team plan, 8, 9, 78–79
Dry run simulation, 64

Effective leadership, 4, 33, 67–68

Force field chart, 33–34, 88

Getting ready *see* Preparation
Goals, 3, 12, 14, 32
Groundrules, 7–8

Ideas, 39–46
  decision checklist, 40
  team building, 40–41
  tools and processes, 41–45
Implementation checklist, 68, 69
Implementation plan, 67–71
Implementation timetable, 48, 54–55, 98
Inconsistent practices, 24, 36, 90
Interrelationship worksheet, 40, 42–44, 92

Job descriptions, 48, 53

Leadership, 4, 33, 67–68
Leadership roles diagram, 23, 29–31, 87
Leadership roles worksheet, 47, 52–53, 96

Mazda reengineering, 11
Mission, 4–6
  see also Design team charter

Network diagram, 23, 24, 26–28, 85

Organizational options, 24, 34–36, 57, 89

Plans
  action, 61–62, 100
  communication, 68, 70, 101
  design team, 8, 9, 78–79
  training, 47, 53, 54, 97
  troubleshooting, 63–65
PMI chart and organizational options, 24, 34–36, 57, 89
Preparation, 1–10
  decision checklist, 1–2
  team building, 2–4
  tools and processes, 4–8
Process diagram, 11, 12, 14–16, 80–81
Processes *see* specific tools and processes, e.g., Cost/benefit analysis
Proposal worksheet, 59–61, 99

Recommendations, 47–55
  decision checklist, 48, 49
  team building, 48, 50
  tools and processes, 48–55
Related changes *see* Associated changes; Changes
Responsibility chart, 23, 28–29, 30, 86
Responsibility matrix, 47, 51–52, 95
Results-oriented team structure, 3, 32, 40, 44, 58–59

Shared goals, 3, 12, 14, 32
Sign-up sheet, 47, 48, 50–51, 94
Social analysis, 23–37
  decision checklist, 24, 25
  team building, 24, 26
  tools and processes, 24, 26–36
Staff commitment, 4, 32, 63–64
Stakeholders, 6
Standards of excellence, 2–4, 32
Starting up *see* Getting ready
Steering committee, 1, 4, 36–37, 40, 44, 71
Structure, 3, 32, 40, 44, 58–59
Supportive systems, 3, 24, 26, 33

Team assessment, 23, 32–34, 36
Team-building activity
  collaborative climate, 3, 48, 50
  committed staff, 4, 63–64
  competent members, 3, 40–41
  effective leadership, 4, 67–68
  shared goals, 3, 12, 14, 32
  standards of excellence, 2–4, 32
  structure, 3, 32, 40, 44, 58–59
  supportive systems, 3, 24, 26, 33
Technical analysis, 11–22
  decision checklist, 12, 13
  team building, 12, 14
  tools and processes, 12–22
Tools *see* specific tools and processes, e.g., Cost/benefit analysis
Training plan, 47, 53, 54, 97
Troubleshooting, 63–65

Variance matrix, 11, 18, 20, 83

Weighted criteria chart, 40–42, 57, 91
Work flow diagram, 11, 16–17